Angel Kisses
And
Snuggle-Time Prayers

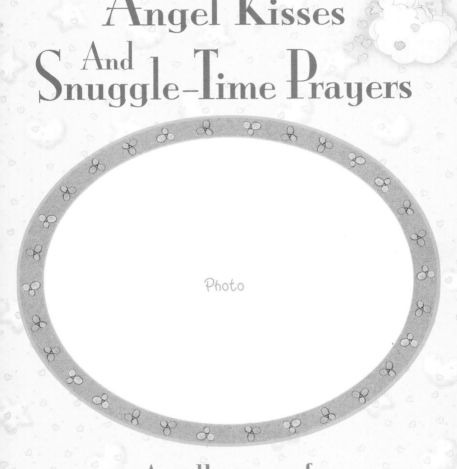

Photo

A collection of
Verses, Prayers, and Quiet
Moments of Love

How precious also are Your thoughts to me,
O God! How great is the sum of them!
If I should count them, they would be
more in number than the sand;
When I awake, I am still with You.

Psalm 139:17–18

The last ray of sun has disappeared over the horizon.
The telltale signs of sleepy eyes and dragging feet remind
you the time has come. Bedtime for your little one awaits, and
you know the ritual well. First a bath, then brushing, and a
book or two. At last comes your favorite part—the final
tuck-in with tons of kisses and hugs. You want them to know
just how special they are. How their smile lights up your day.
How the touch of their tiny hand melts your heart.

You also want them to know how
important they are to God. *Angel Kisses
And Snuggle-Time Prayers* makes it
easy through the select Scripture
and prayer portions alongside Sam
Butcher's beloved bedtime illustra-
tions. Complete with space for family
photos and a section to record your
prayer and theirs, it is the perfect way to
tell them God's truth, show them His
love, and teach them ways to trust
and pray that will take them not only
through the night, but through the rest
of life, as well.

Now I lay me down to sleep;

I pray the Lord my soul to keep,

while angels watch me

through the night, 'til I awake

in morning's light.

Amen

This Book Belongs To Me

Mikaela Renee Alwine
Name

Aunt Lucille and Renée
Given By

December 2004
Date

First Birthday
Occasion

Special People
I Love

Photo

My Parents

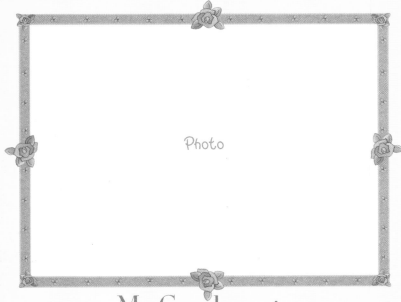

Photo

My Grandparents

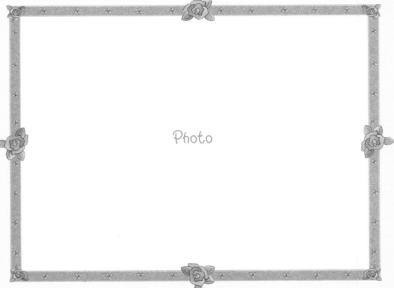

Photo

My Babysitter

Things That Make Me Happy

List some items that make your child feel happy, safe, and loved!
(family, pets, places, friends, special toys)

_____   _____

_____   _____

_____   _____

_____   _____

_____   _____

Photo of a special pet,
or place or friend.

For He shall give His angels charge over you, to keep you in all your ways.

Psalm 91:11

From the moment they wake up until they're safely tucked in bed, good parents are on guard. "Be careful," or "Hold my hand" are just some of the phrases repeated over and over in an attempt to keep active and inexperienced explorers "boo-boo" free. It's an endless job, often filled with anxiety and stress—unless we learn one of God's key secrets that He'd like us to pass on to our little ones.

God really is the one in control. We plan. We prepare. We do our best to prevent. But He holds our future in His hands, and He watches over us every step of the way. Tonight, as you tuck your tiny treasure in bed, remind them that even while they sleep, God sees them. Even while they're deep in dreams, His angels are holding them close. It's a secret comfort only God's children can know; in the understanding comes a peace that sweetens both the night and day. As you read each evening from *Angel Kisses And Snuggle-Time Prayers,* may the poignant pictures and thoughtfully selected Scriptures become a tangible expression of God's loving embrace that envelops both you and your child tonight and always.

For I know
the thoughts that
I think toward you,
says the LORD,
thoughts of peace
and not of evil,
to give you a future
and a hope.

Jeremiah 29:11

Since you were
precious in
My sight,
you have
been honored,
and I have
loved you.

Isaiah 43:4

The LORD has
appeared of old
to me, saying:
"Yes, I have loved
you with an
everlasting love;
therefore with
lovingkindness
I have drawn you."

Jeremiah 31:3

For God so loved the world that He gave His only begotten Son, that whoever believes in Him should not perish but have everlasting life.

John 3:16

The LORD your God
in your midst,
The Mighty One,
will save;
He will rejoice
over you with gladness,
He will quiet you
with His love,
He will rejoice
over you with singing.

Zephaniah 3:17

In this is love, not
that we loved God,
but that He loved us
and sent His Son...
for our sins. Beloved
if God so loved us,
we also ought to love
one another.

1 John 4:10, 11

And we have known and believed the love that God has for us. God is love, and he who abides in love abides in God, and God in him.

1 John 4:16

The LORD bless you
and keep you;
The LORD make His face
shine upon you, and be
gracious to you;
The LORD lift up His
countenance upon you,
and give you peace.

Numbers 6:24–26

Be of
good courage,
and He shall
strengthen
your heart,
all you who hope
in the LORD.

Psalm 31:24

I sought
the LORD,
and He heard me,
and delivered
me from all
my fears.

Psalm 34:4

Be strong and of good
courage, do not fear
nor be afraid of them;
for the LORD your
God, He is the One
who goes with you.
He will not leave you
nor forsake you.

Deuteronomy 31:6

Our soul
waits for the LORD;
He is our help
and our shield.
For our heart
shall rejoice in Him,
Because we have
trusted in His holy name.
Let Your mercy,
O LORD, be upon us,
Just as we hope in You.

Psalm 33:20-22

Be anxious for nothing,
but in everything by prayer
and supplication, with
thanksgiving, let your
requests be made known
to God; and the peace of
God which surpasses all
understanding, will guard
your hearts and minds
through Christ Jesus.

Philippians 4:6, 7

My little children, let us not love in word or in tongue, but in deed and in truth. And by this we know that we are of the truth, and shall assure our hearts before Him.

1 John 3:18, 19

Continue earnestly in prayer, being vigilant in it with thanksgiving.

Colossians 4:2

Rejoice always, pray without ceasing, in everything give thanks; for this is the will of God in Christ Jesus for you.

1 Thessalonians 5:16, 17

I will say
of the LORD,
"He is my refuge
and my fortress;
my God, in Him
I will trust."

Psalm 91:2

I will both lie
down in peace,
and sleep;
for You alone,
O LORD,
make me dwell
in safety.

Psalm 4:8

A Special Prayer to Me From Those Who Love Me the Most....

(Parents, grandparents, family...
take a moment to write a prayer of comfort and love
for your little one as you tuck them into bed.)

My Own
Bedtime Prayer

(Help write down your little one's special words of prayer...
their blessings, joys, hopes and dreams!)

_____

_____

_____

_____

_____

_____

_____

_____

_____

_____

_____

_____

_____

Amen